LEARN TO READ DRUM MUSIC

Book 1

Andy Green

Dedicated to my wife Caz, my best friend in the whole wide world.

With grateful thanks to my family, friends and colleagues for their invaluable help and support.

Published by Agogo Publishing - www.agogopublishing.co.uk

ISBN 978 0 9927685 0 8

Printed in the United Kingdom.

Introduction

Imagine for a moment that you had never learnt to read or write. Think how difficult life would be and how much you would miss out on. Being able to read drum music is just the same. You don't have to learn it (and lots of drummers don't) but if you can it opens up a whole new world.

Written drum music can help you to learn new pieces, grooves, fills and solos much more quickly and easily. There are also lots of bands and groups around that only use written music. If you can't read then you can't play with these groups!

The good news is that this book should get you reading drum music very quickly. All you have to do is read the short explanations, complete the exercises and discuss anything that you don't understand with your teacher. You can also use the 'play' exercises to try out what you have learnt on the drum kit.

Here's what some of the different sections of the book look like:

Exercise

Throughout the book there are lots of short exercises for you to do.

Review

Review sections test you on everything you have learnt so far.

Play!

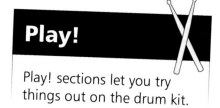

Play! sections let you try things out on the drum kit.

Once you have finished this book don't forget to get hold of book 2 to learn some of the more advanced features of drum notation.

Good luck!

Andy Green
BA (Hons) Music & Popular Music

Notes for teachers

These books were written to try and make sense of what, at times, can be quite a confusing subject. Musical notation is supposed to be there to help us, yet for the young drummer it can often prove quite daunting.

The many different notational styles that composers, arrangers and educators have used over the years means that a symbol used in one book can mean something entirely different in another. For that reason, this book aims to teach drummers how to interpret any style of percussion notation, regardless of which method has been used.

The material is designed so that a few pages can be set as homework each week. A small amount of lesson time can then be used for marking the exercises; going over anything the student doesn't understand and hearing them play through the 'Play' exercises.

For further information and resources please visit:

www.readdrummusic.com

Please don't photocopy this book and remember that a minimum of 50p will be donated to Teenage Cancer Trust for each copy sold

Contents

Tick each section off as you complete it.

Musical ingredients

Music is made up of lots of different ingredients that all have their own particular job to do. For example, some control how fast a piece of music is, whilst others control how loud the notes are.

This book will look at all of the important ingredients and see how they fit together, starting with **pulse**, **beats** and **notes**.

Pulse

Every piece of music has a **pulse**.

This is like a heartbeat, and it is what makes you tap your foot along to the music.

Drummers use the pulse to keep them strictly in time with other musicians.

Beat

Each tap of your foot is called a **beat** and lots of beats together make a pulse.

Beats don't actually make any sound, they are just imaginary.

Counting

It is really important that you count along to each beat of the pulse, as otherwise you can easily get lost in the song.

'1'   '2'   '3'   '4'

Fast and slow pulses

If the beats are closer together then the pulse is **faster**, but if the beats are further apart then the pulse is **slower**.

This is a **fast** pulse, as the beats are really close together:

This is a **medium** pulse, as the beats are a moderate distance apart:

This is a **slow** pulse, as the beats are much further apart:

Notes

Notes are the symbols that tell you when to play a sound and how long to make it last for. They come in all shapes and sizes and you will learn lots more about them later.

Try and remember that beats are just the imaginary things you count, whereas notes actually tell you when to play a sound. Sometimes notes happen at the same time as each beat of the pulse, however, other times they happen in-between the beats...

'On the beat'

Sometimes notes are **on the beat**. This means they sound at exactly the same time as each beat of the pulse.

'Off the beat'

Sometimes notes are **off the beat**. This means they sound in-between each beat of the pulse.

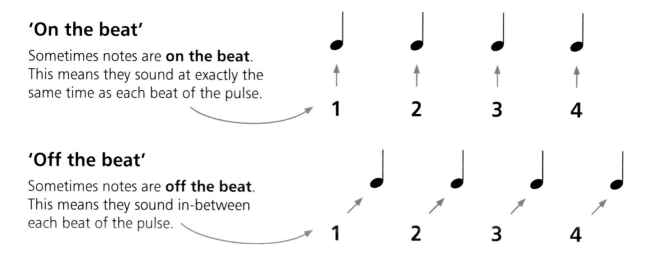

If this all seems a bit confusing then try counting the beats and clapping the notes. Try and clap some that are 'on the beat' and some that are 'off the beat'.

Exercise 1

Fill in the gaps using the words in the box.
Cross each one off as you use it.

E.g. Lots of ....beats........ make up a pulse.

Box of words:
~~beats~~   beats   count   pulse   slow   play   fast   off the beat   pulse

1. You need to .... each beat of the pulse as otherwise you might get lost.

2. A .... piece of music has beats that are close together.

3. The heartbeat of a piece of music can be called a ....

4. A .... piece of music has beats that are far apart.

5. Notes tell you when to .... , whereas .... are what you count.

6. The .... can help you to keep in time with other musicians.

7. Notes that are played in-between beats of the pulse are ....

Lines and spaces

Now you know what notes look like, you need to know where to put them!

Stave

Notes live on a group of five lines, called a **stave**. If there are five lines, then that must mean there are four spaces in-between:

Some notes go on the lines, whilst others go in the spaces. Later on in the book you will learn more about which ones go where.

note on a line   note in a space

Exercise 2

Draw a note on the correct **line** for each of the staves below. Use a black dot like the one in the example.

E.g.   1.   2.   3.   4.

2nd line up   bottom line   top line   4th line up   3rd line up

Exercise 3

Draw a note in the correct **space** for each of the staves below.

1.   2.   3.   4.

top space   3rd space up   bottom space   2nd space up

The percussion clef

At the start of each stave you will usually see a **percussion clef**. This is an important symbol as it tells you that the music is for drums or percussion.

There are other types of clefs as well, although these are very rarely used for drum kit music.

Exercise 4

1. Using a ruler, have a go at drawing a stave in the space below. Use the dots as a guide.

2. Add a percussion clef at the beginning.

3. Add some notes on lines and in spaces.

Exercise 5

Fill in the gaps using the words in the box.
Cross each one off as you use it.

> percussion   four   space   clef
>   five
> on the beat   stave   line

1. Notes live on a ....

2. Drum music has a .... clef at the start of each stave.

3. A stave has .... lines and .... spaces.

4. A percussion .... is important as it tells you that the music is for drums/percussion.

5. Sometimes notes are on a .... and sometimes they are in a ....

6. Notes that are played at the same time as the pulse are ....

Bars

Some songs can be over 1,000 beats long! It would be very difficult to count from one to 1,000, so the music is split up into 'boxes'. Each box is called a **bar**:

Bar-line

The lines in-between each bar are called **bar-lines**:

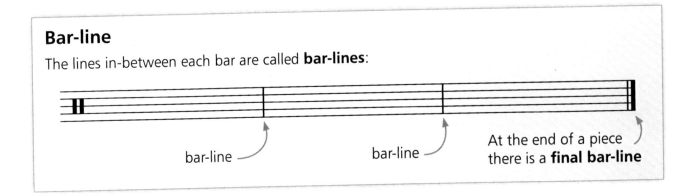

bar-line   bar-line   At the end of a piece there is a **final bar-line**

In most of the music that you are likely to play there will be four beats in each bar. This means that all you need to do is count from one to four over and over again.

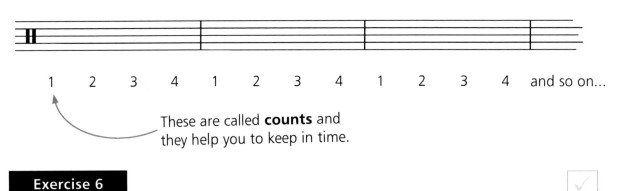

1 2 3 4   1 2 3 4   1 2 3 4   and so on...

These are called **counts** and they help you to keep in time.

Exercise 6   ✓

Add the counts to these pieces of music, then draw in the bar-lines, making sure that each bar has four counts. The first bar has been done for you.

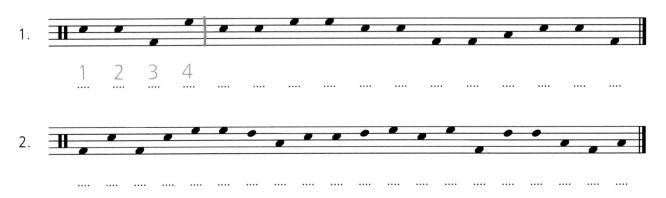

In book 2 you will learn about music that has two, three, six, nine or twelve beats per bar! However, this is less common so for now you can stick to pieces that have four beats in each bar.

Notes

Notes tell you which part of the drum kit to play and how long to make the sound last for. Some notes last a long time whilst others finish really quickly.

The length of a note is measured in beats, so a long note might last for several beats, whilst a short note might last for a fraction of a beat. You will start by learning some of the longer notes:

Semibreve

The **semibreve** lasts for four beats.

 = 4 beats

Start counting the semibreve as soon as the note sounds and don't stop until the end of the fourth beat.

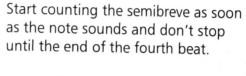

Minim

The **minim** lasts for two beats.

 = 2 beats

Start counting the minim as soon as the note sounds and don't stop until the end of the second beat.

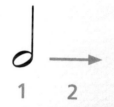

Keep counting!

Drums usually make quite short sounds that die away really quickly. However, it is important that you keep on counting for the full length of the note, even if the sound dies away.

Exercise 7 ✓

Copy these semibreves and minims and then fill in the missing words.

1.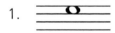

   This is a ....

   It lasts for .... beats.

2.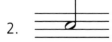

   This is a ....

   It lasts for .... beats.

3.

   Here there are two ....

   In total they last for .... beats.

Rests

Music would be really boring if it went on and on without stopping. This is why **rests** are used, which mean 'be silent' or 'have a rest'. Just like with notes, there are lots of different kinds of rests.

Semibreve rest

 = 4 beats

The **semibreve rest** tells you to be silent for four beats. It is basically just a black box that hangs down from the fourth line up.

Semibreve rests are drawn in the middle of the bar:

Minim rest

 = 2 beats

The **minim rest** tells you to be silent for two beats. It is a black box that sits on the third line up.

If you can't remember which rest goes on which line, think '**middle = minim**'.

This will help you to work out that the minim rest goes on the middle line.

Don't forget! Semibreve and minim rests don't need a line - just a box!

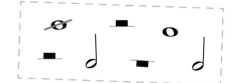

Exercise 8

Fill each gap with a suitable note or rest from the box so that each bar adds up to four beats in total. Remember that some notes last for four beats whilst others last for two beats. You can decide which line or space the notes go in.

Exercise 9

Add up the value of these notes and rests to calculate the total number of beats.

E.g. $\quad \downarrow + \blacksquare = 4$ beats

1. $\mathbf{o}$ + $\downarrow$ = ... beat(s)

2. $\blacksquare$ + $\mathbf{o}$ = ... beat(s)

3. $\downarrow$ + $\blacksquare$ = ... beat(s)

4. $\mathbf{o}$ + $\downarrow$ + $\blacksquare$ = ... beat(s)

5. $\blacksquare$ + $\blacksquare$ + $\blacksquare$ = ... beat(s)

6. $\mathbf{o}$ + $\blacksquare$ + $\blacksquare$ + $\blacksquare$ = ... beat(s)

Play! No.1

Have a go at playing these short pieces on the snare drum. Keep a steady pulse and don't forget to count!

1 2 3 4 1 2 3 4 1 2 3 4 1 2 3 4

1 2 3 4 1 2 3 4 1 2 3 4 1 2 3 4

1 2 3 4 1 2 3 4 1 2 3 4 1 2 3 4

1 2 3 4 1 2 3 4 1 2 3 4 1 2 3 4

Crotchets

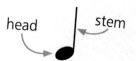

So far you have learnt about minims and semibreves. The next note you need to look at is the **crotchet**. This is probably the most important note, as one crotchet lasts for one beat.

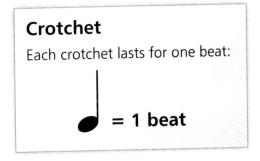

Crotchet

Each crotchet lasts for one beat:

= 1 beat

Heads and stems

Each crotchet is made up of a black dot and a straight line.

The dot is known as a 'head' or 'notehead' and the line is called a stem.

head   stem

Sometimes the stem goes up and sometimes it goes down. When the stem is up it is positioned to the right of the notehead and when the stem is down it is positioned to the left.

to the right

stem up

to the left

stem down

Exercise 10

Draw **one or more crotchets** in each bar so that they all last for four beats. You can choose which line or space, but make sure their stems are **up**.

1.   2.   3.

1   2   3   4

Do the same with these bars, but this time draw your crotchets with their stems **down**.

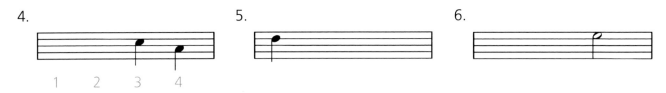

4.   5.   6.

1   2   3   4

Add a **crotchet**, **minim** or **semibreve** into each of these gaps, making sure each bar lasts for four beats. This time you can choose whether the stems are up or down. Remember that semibreves do not need a stem!

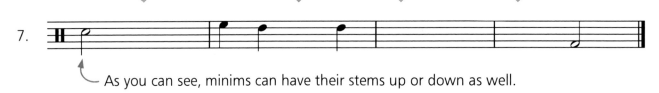

7.

As you can see, minims can have their stems up or down as well.

Stems up or stems down?

You will find out more about when to point the stems up and when to point them down later on in the book. For now draw them all with their stems up.

Crotchet rests

Just like minims and semibreves, crotchets also have their own rests.

Crotchet rest

The **crotchet rest** lasts for one whole beat and it is completely silent.

= 1 beat

It is drawn across the middle three lines like this:

Exercise 11

Try drawing some crotchet rests on the stave below. Use four strokes of your pen/pencil and make sure the last one is a curve. Use the dots to help you with the first two.

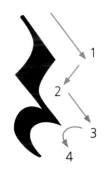

1.   2.   3.   4.

Don't worry if yours doesn't look exactly like the example!

Exercise 12

Fill in the gaps below.

1. 𝅝   is called a .... and lasts for .... beat(s)

2. ▬   is called a .... and lasts for .... beat(s)

3. 𝅗𝅥   is called a .... and lasts for .... beat(s)

4. ▬   is called a .... and lasts for .... beat(s)

5. ♩   is called a .... and lasts for .... beat(s)

6. 𝄽   is called a .... and lasts for .... beat(s)

13

These exercises will help you to remember the difference between all the notes and rests that you have learnt so far.

Draw in the bar-lines for these pieces of music so that each bar lasts for four beats.
The first bar-line has been done for you.

1.

2.

3.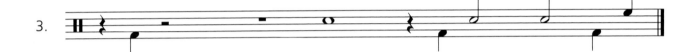

4.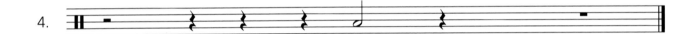

5.

Add up the value of these notes and rests to calculate the total number of beats.

E.g. ♩ + ▬ = 3 beats

1. ♩ + ♩ + 𝄽 = ... beat(s)

2. 𝅝 + 𝅗𝅥 = ... beat(s)

3. ▬ + ♩ = ... beat(s)

4. ▬ + 𝄽 + 𝄽 = ... beat(s)

5. ▬ + 𝅝 + 𝅝 = ... beat(s)

6. 𝄽 + 𝅗𝅥 + ▬ + ♩ = ... beat(s)

14

Exercise 15

Fill each gap with one of the **notes or rests** you have learnt so far. You can decide which line or space the notes go in but make sure each bar adds up to four beats.

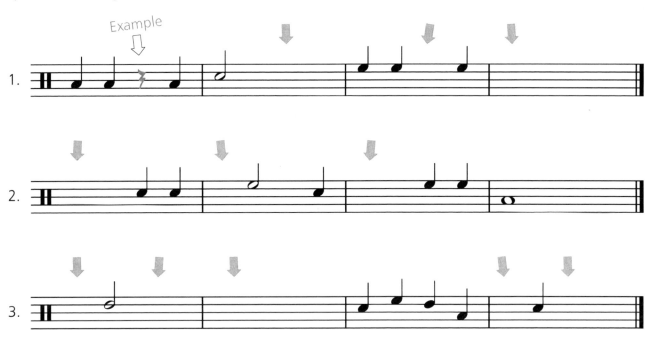

Play! No.2

Try playing these pieces on the snare drum. Each one uses a variety of notes and rests so it is important to count really carefully.

Time signatures

As well as notes and rests there are lots of other important signs and symbols used in drum music. One of these is the **time signature**.

The time signature

A **time signature** tells you how many beats there are in each bar. The most common one looks like this:

It tells us that there are four crotchet beats in each bar of music.

The time signature appears just after the clef on the first line of music and is pronounced 'four four'.

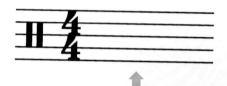

Have a go at drawing one on the stave above. You can use normal 4s, they don't have to be fancy!

Exercise 16

Add a time signature to each of these pieces of music. Then add bar-lines so that each bar has the correct number of beats.

Common time

$\frac{4}{4}$ is the most common type of time signature and because of this it is sometimes called **common time** instead.

Common time is shown with a letter C.

Sometimes you will see $\frac{4}{4}$, whilst other times you will see a **C** for common time.

Just remember that they both mean the same thing - four beats in each bar.

There are lots of other kinds of time signatures as well, such as $\frac{3}{4}$, $\frac{6}{8}$, $\frac{2}{2}$ etc. Time signatures will be explained in much more detail in Book 2.

16

Review 1

Read through the music then answer the questions below...

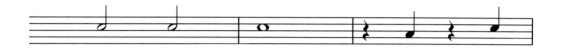

1. There are .... beats in each bar.

2. One of the bar-lines is missing on the bottom line of music - draw it in.

3. There is a total of .... crotchet notes in the piece above.

4. Draw a percussion clef at the beginning of the music so that you know that this piece is for drums.

5. There are .... bars in the piece in total.

6. Draw a circle around all of the minim rests.

7. Three minims last for .... beats in total.

8. There is a total of .... semibreve notes in the piece above.

9. Draw a time signature on the first line of music.

10. There is a total of .... crotchet rests in the piece above.

Total

/10

Drums

So far you have seen lots of different types of notes. Now you need to know where on the stave they belong.

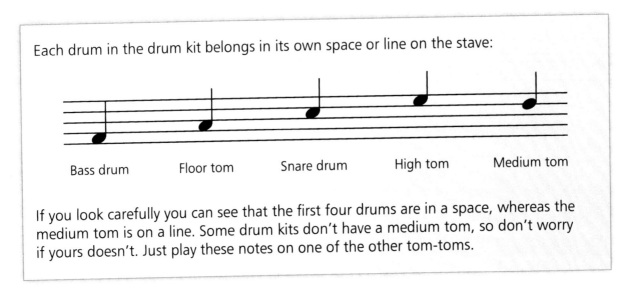

Each drum in the drum kit belongs in its own space or line on the stave:

Bass drum   Floor tom   Snare drum   High tom   Medium tom

If you look carefully you can see that the first four drums are in a space, whereas the medium tom is on a line. Some drum kits don't have a medium tom, so don't worry if yours doesn't. Just play these notes on one of the other tom-toms.

It is really important that you learn where each drum goes, so there will be lots of exercises throughout this book to help you remember. If you get stuck, remember that the drums go up the stave in order of size. So, the bass drum (the biggest) is at the bottom, and the high tom (the smallest) is at the top.

Exercise 17

Label the drum kit by drawing the correct note on the stave (use crotchets). Then write its name on the line underneath. The snare drum has been done for you.

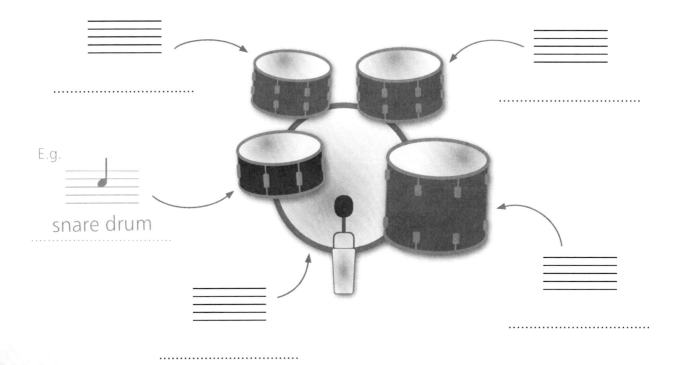

E.g.

snare drum

18

Big Fish Swim Home

If you find it difficult to remember which drum goes where, try saying the phrase 'Big Fish Swim Home'.

The first letter of each word is the same as the first letter of each drum.

Home	→	**H**igh tom
Swim	→	**S**nare drum
Fish	→	**F**loor tom
Big	→	**B**ass drum

As for the medium tom, just remember that this is the only drum written on a line.

Exercise 18

Which drum should you play each of these notes on?

1.

....

2.

....

3.

....

4.

....

5.

....

6.

....

7.

....

8.

....

Exercise 19

Draw the correct note in the correct place on the stave. The first one has been done for you.

E.g.

High tom
(crotchet)

1.

Bass drum
(semibreve)

2.

Floor tom
(minim)

3.

Snare drum
(semibreve)

4.

Medium tom
(minim)

5.

Snare drum
(crotchet)

6.

High tom
(semibreve)

7.

Bass drum
(minim)

19

Cymbals

There are lots of different ways to show cymbals. This is because people that write drum music can't agree on which way is best! You will learn what some people call the **standard** method first and then look at some variations on this later.

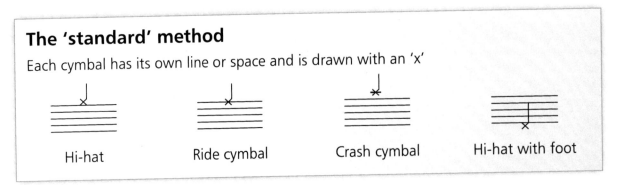

The 'standard' method
Each cymbal has its own line or space and is drawn with an 'x'

Hi-hat   Ride cymbal   Crash cymbal   Hi-hat with foot

Exercise 20

Label the cymbals by drawing the correct note on the stave, then writing its name on the line underneath. Use 'x' notes like the ones above.

Exercise 21

Name these drums and cymbals.

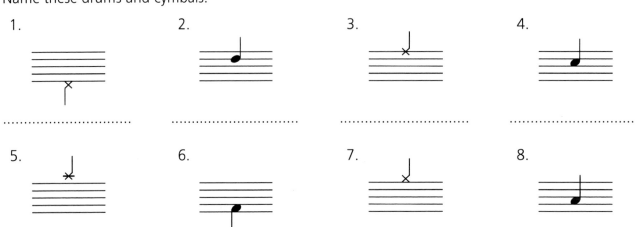

1.

2.

3.

4.

5.

6.

7.

8.

Exercise 22

Draw the correct note in the correct place on the stave.

1.

2.

3.

4.

Crash cymbal
(crotchet)

Floor tom
(semibreve)

Bass drum
(minim)

Hi-hat with foot
(crotchet)

5.

6.

7.

8.

Hi-hat
(crotchet)

Medium tom
(semibreve)

High tom
(minim)

Ride cymbal
(crotchet)

9.

10.

11.

12.

Snare drum
(minim)

Bass drum
(semibreve)

Medium tom
(crotchet)

Floor tom
(crotchet)

Longer notes

Cymbals that last for longer than one beat are often written as a crotchet, followed by a number of rests.

1 beat

2 beats

3 beats

4 beats

Exercise 23

Draw one or more **rests** after each cymbal so that each bar lasts for 4 beats.

1.

2.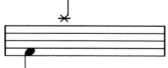

3.

4.

5.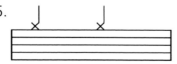

6.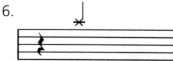

Cymbal variations

So far you have learnt the 'standard' method of writing cymbals. To keep things simple, this is the method that will be used throughout this book. There are, however, several other ways to write cymbals and it is important that you know how some of these work.

Labels

Sometimes **labels** are used to describe each cymbal. This means that the cymbals are all drawn with an **X** note-head in the same place on top of the stave. The name of the cymbal is then written just above it, so that you know which one to play.

Name of cymbal goes here

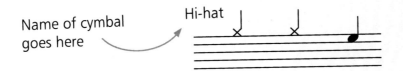

Often the names are shortened to **HH** (Hi-hat), **RC** (Ride cymbal) and **CC** (Crash cymbal). As you can see, all of the cymbal notes below look exactly the same. It is just their labels that are different:

Shapes

Yet another way of writing cymbals is to use different shapes for different cymbals.

For example, quite often the crash cymbal will be drawn as an **X** with a circle around it, or sometimes a triangle or another shape might be used instead.

The example below starts with a crash cymbal note and then moves to the hi-hat for the rest of the bar.

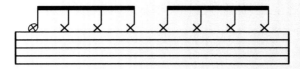

The only way to know which shape is used for which cymbal is to look at the key....

Using the key

Drum music could get really confusing with all these different methods in use. To make things clearer, a **key** is often used.

A key is a diagram, like the ones below, that tells you exactly how each drum and cymbal will be shown. They are usually found at the front or back of a drum book and sometimes they might be called a **legend** instead. There is a key at the back of this book, so have a look at this if you get stuck.

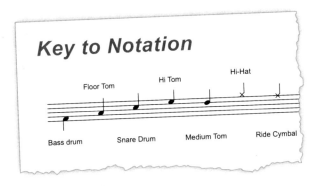

What if there isn't a key?

If there isn't a key, or if you are confused, then simply use your common sense and musical ear to decide which drum or cymbal to play. Usually there is no right or wrong answer, so in this case you can interpret the music in the way that you think sounds best.

Play! No.3

These pieces use lots of different drums and cymbals. If you get stuck, have a look at the key at the back of this book.

23

Quavers

So far you have looked at notes that last for one beat or more. There are some, however, that last for less than a beat. One of these is the **quaver**.

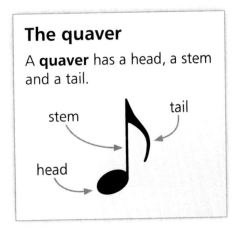

The quaver

A **quaver** has a head, a stem and a tail.

stem

tail

head

Sometimes the stems are up, and sometimes they are down.

Stem up

Stem down

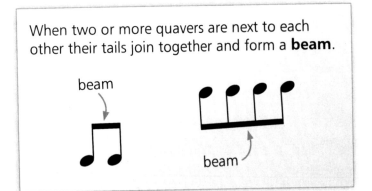

When two or more quavers are next to each other their tails join together and form a **beam**.

beam

beam

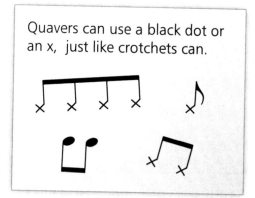

Quavers can use a black dot or an x, just like crotchets can.

Exercise 24

Copy these notes.

1.  COPY

2.  COPY

3.  COPY

4.  COPY

5.  COPY

6.  COPY

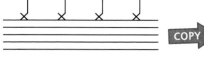

A quaver lasts for half a beat.

= ½ **beat**

If you add two halves together you make a whole.

½ + ½ = 1

This means that two quavers 'added together' last for one whole beat in total.

♪ + ♪ = **1 beat**

Exercise 25

Add up each of the fractions below. This will help you to get used to different types of note lengths.

E.g. 1 + 1 + ½ = 2½

1. ½ + ½ = ...

2. 1 + ½ = ...

3. ½ + ½ + ½ = ...

4. ½ + 1 + ½ = ...

Quavers look a little different when they are beamed together, but remember that each one is still a separate note that lasts for half a beat.

Here there are **two separate** quavers that last for 1 whole beat in total.

Here there are **four separate** quavers that last for 2 whole beats in total.

Exercise 26

Add up the value of these notes to calculate the total number of beats.

E.g. ♩ + ♪ = 1½ beats

1. ♫ = ... beat(s)

2. ♩ + ♫ = ... beat(s)

3. ♪ + ♪ + ♪ + ♪ = ... beat(s)

4. ♫ + ♪ = ... beat(s)

5. ♫♫ + ♫ = ... beat(s)

6. 𝅝 + ♪ = ... beat(s)

Counting quavers

Instead of just counting '1 2 3 4', it can be really helpful to say 'and' in-between each number. This will help you to hear exactly when to play the quavers that are in-between the beats.

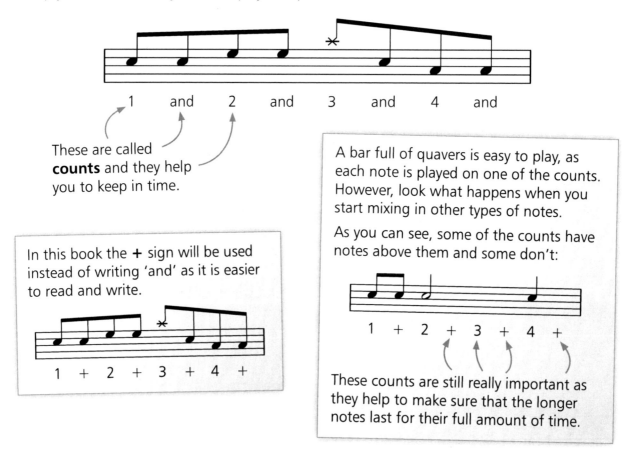

1   and   2   and   3   and   4   and

These are called **counts** and they help you to keep in time.

In this book the **+** sign will be used instead of writing 'and' as it is easier to read and write.

1 + 2 + 3 + 4 +

A bar full of quavers is easy to play, as each note is played on one of the counts. However, look what happens when you start mixing in other types of notes.

As you can see, some of the counts have notes above them and some don't:

1 + 2 + 3 + 4 +

These counts are still really important as they help to make sure that the longer notes last for their full amount of time.

Here are some examples of how different types of notes can be counted:

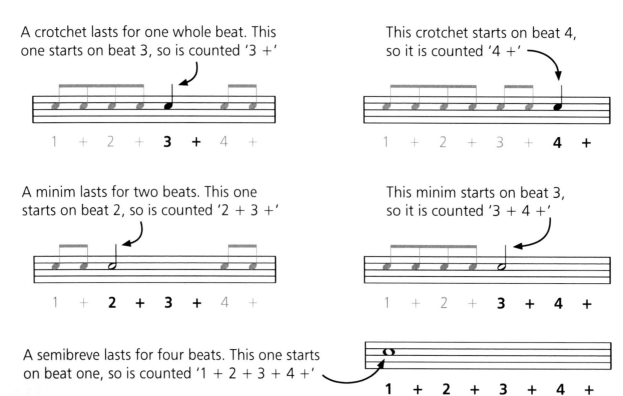

A crotchet lasts for one whole beat. This one starts on beat 3, so is counted '3 +'

1 + 2 + **3 + 4** +

This crotchet starts on beat 4, so it is counted '4 +'

1 + 2 + 3 + **4 +**

A minim lasts for two beats. This one starts on beat 2, so is counted '2 + 3 +'

1 + **2 + 3 +** 4 +

This minim starts on beat 3, so it is counted '3 + 4 +'

1 + 2 + **3 + 4 +**

A semibreve lasts for four beats. This one starts on beat one, so is counted '1 + 2 + 3 + 4 +'

1 + 2 + 3 + 4 +

Exercise 27

Carefully re-write each of these rhythms above the correct counts. Remember that some of the counts won't have any notes above them. The first one has been done for you.

E.g.
1 + 2 + 3 + 4 +

1.
1 + 2 + 3 + 4 +

2.
1 + 2 + 3 + 4 +

3.
1 + 2 + 3 + 4 +

4.
1 + 2 + 3 + 4 +

5.
1 + 2 + 3 + 4 +

Beaming quavers

If the time signature of the music is 4/4 or Common time (like all the music in this book) then quavers can be beamed together in groups of **up to half a bar**.

That means two, three or four notes.

The **beam** is the thick black line that joins the notes together

Exercise 28

Mark each one of these examples with a tick ✓ if they are beamed correctly or a cross ✗ if they are beamed wrongly.

1. 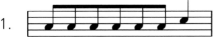 ☐
2.  ☐
3. 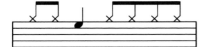 ☐
4. 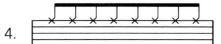 ☐
5.  ☐
6.  ☐

Play! No.4

These pieces use lots of crotchets and quavers. To help you stay in time, make sure you count the 'and' in-between each beat.

1 + 2 + 3 + 4 +   1 + 2 + 3 + 4 +   1 + 2 + 3 + 4 +   1 + 2 + 3 + 4 +

1 + 2 + 3 + 4 +   1 + 2 + 3 + 4 +   1 + 2 + 3 + 4 +   1 + 2 + 3 + 4 +

Quaver rests

Just like all the other notes, quavers also have their own rests.

> ## Quaver rest
> This is a **quaver rest**. It means to be silent for half a beat:
>
> = **half a beat of silence**

> This is what it looks like on the stave:
>
>

Exercise 29

Try drawing some quaver rests below. Start with a dot, then a curve and then a straight, diagonal line. Use the dots to help you with the first two.

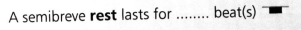

1.   2.   3.   4.

Exercise 30

Here are all the notes and rests you have learnt so far. See if you can fill in the blanks.

> ## Semibreves
> A semibreve lasts for .... beat(s)
>
> A semibreve **rest** lasts for .... beat(s)

> ## Minims
> A minim lasts for .... beat(s)
>
> A minim **rest** lasts for .... beat(s)

> ## Crotchets
> A crotchet lasts for .... beat(s)
>
> A crotchet **rest** lasts for .... beat(s)

> ## Quavers
> A quaver lasts for .... a beat
>
> A quaver **rest** lasts for .... a beat

Add up the value of these notes and rests to calculate the total number of beats.

E.g. ♪ + 𝄾 = 1½ beats

1. ♪ + 𝄾 = ... beat(s)

2. 𝄾 + 𝅝 = ... beat(s)

3. 𝄾 + 𝅗𝅥 = ... beat(s)

4. ♫ + 𝄻 + 𝄾 = ... beat(s)

5. 𝄽 + 𝄾 + 𝄾 = ... beat(s)

6. 𝄾 + 𝄻 + 𝄽 + 𝅗𝅥 = ... beat(s)

Fill each of the gaps below with **one** of the **rests** that you have learnt so far. Make sure that each bar lasts for four whole beats. The first one has been done for you.

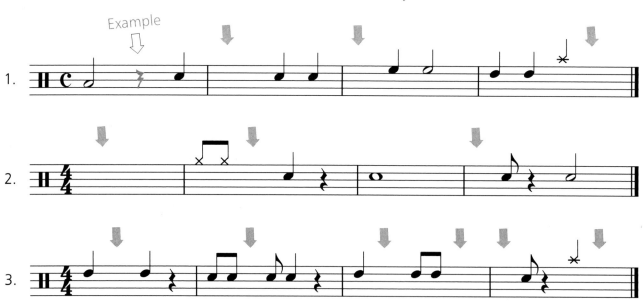

Now fill each of these gaps with **one** of the **notes** you have learnt so far. Make sure each bar lasts for four beats.

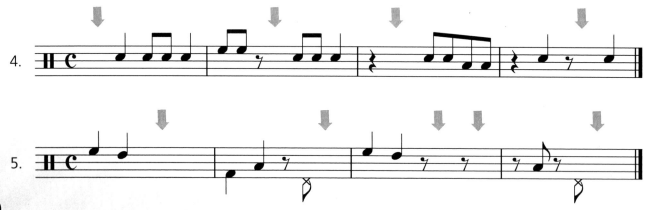

30

Review 2

Read through the music then answer the questions below...

1. The .... is the cymbal that is used the most in this piece.

2. Add a time signature to the first bar.

3. A .... is a diagram that tells us which line or space each drum and cymbal will be written on.

4. Draw a note in the third bar so that it adds up to four beats.

5. Four quavers last for .... beat(s) in total.

6. Draw a circle around the group of quavers that are not beamed correctly.

7. The 'heartbeat' of a piece of music is called the ....

8. Draw in the missing bar-lines on the third line of music.

9. In bar number .... the notes are all 'off the beat'.

10. Draw in the missing Percussion clef on line 2.

Total

/10

Tempo

Music can be fast, slow or any number of different speeds in-between. The word **tempo** is used to describe how fast or slow the musical pulse is. For example, some pieces have a slow tempo, whilst others may have a really fast tempo.

Metronome

A **metronome** can be used to help you play at the correct tempo. They come in all shapes and sizes and make a 'click' or 'beep' sound for every beat of the pulse.

If you set it to a low number, like 40 it will click very slowly but if you set it to a high number, like 180 it will click very fast.

Metronome mark

To show how fast the tempo is, a **metronome mark** is written at the top of the piece:

$$\text{♩} = 90 \text{ bpm}$$

bpm stands for 'beats per minute', so ♩ = 90 bpm means there are 90 crotchet beats per minute.

In other words, for every minute that goes by there will be 90 beats of music.

The more beats per minute, the faster the tempo:

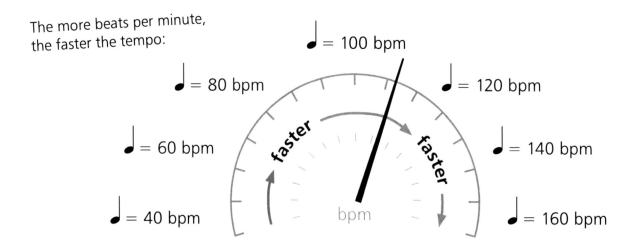

Metronome marks are usually written at the start of the music, just above the time signature.

Sometimes they are called **tempo markings** instead.

The 'bpm' bit is often left out

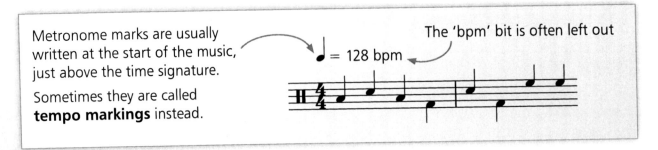

Exercise 33

Fill in the blanks using the words and metronome marks from the box below.

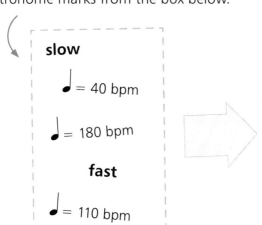

slow

♩ = 40 bpm

♩ = 180 bpm

fast

♩ = 110 bpm

Metronome mark	Meaning
	very fast
♩ = 140 bpm	
	moderate
♩ = 70 bpm	
	very slow

Exercise 34

Write a suitable metronome mark in the correct place above each of these pieces of music.

1.

(very fast)

2.

(slow)

3.

(moderate)

4.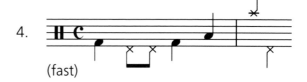

(fast)

Exercise 35

Fill in the gaps using words and symbols from the box.

1. .... describes how fast or slow a piece of music is.

2. 110 bpm is .... than 80 bpm.

3. 50 bpm could be described as a .... tempo.

4. A .... can be used to work out exactly how fast to play.

5. .... means that there are 160 .... beats per ....

Box:
minute
metronome
faster   tempo
slow   crotchet
♩ = 160 bpm

33

Dynamics

pp *f* *mf* *ff*

Drum music becomes much more interesting and creative when played at different volumes. Instructions can be written below the stave to show you when to play loud and when to play soft. These instructions are called **dynamics** and they are based around two Italian words.

Forte means loud in Italian, so the letter **f** is written to indicate a loud section of music. **Piano** (usually pronounced 'pee-ar-no') means soft (or quiet), so the letter **p** is used to indicate a soft section. There are also lots of different degrees of loudness and softness in-between. Try and learn these symbols, Italian words and their meanings:

Softer

Symbol	Italian term	Meaning
ff	fortissimo	very loud
f	forte	loud
mf	mezzo-forte	moderately loud
mp	mezzo-piano	moderately soft
p	piano	soft
pp	pianissimo	very soft

Louder

In other words, 'fairly' loud, but not as loud as forte!

Exercise 36

Write these symbols and terms in order of loudness.

mp   fortissimo   piano   *f*   *pp*

softest

....

loudest

⟸ Getting louder! ⟹

Why are they in Italian?

Lots of the rules about how to write music were made a long time ago in Italy.

Other parts of the world decided that music would be simpler if it had only one main language, so lots of words are still written in Italian.

How long do they last for?

Each dynamic marking carries on until a new one is written.

p   *f*

So in this example the first three notes are soft and the last one is loud.

Gradual changes in volume

Instead of suddenly changing the volume, it can be really dramatic to gradually get louder and louder or softer and softer, little by little. This is shown on the music using the terms **crescendo** and **diminuendo**.

Crescendo

Crescendo means to gradually get louder. Sometimes this is shortened to **cresc.** or shown by drawing a 'hairpin' symbol that gets **wider** towards the end:

Diminuendo

The word **diminuendo** means to gradually get softer. Sometimes this is shortened to **dim.** or shown by drawing a 'hairpin' symbol that gets **narrower** towards the end:

Exercise 37

Draw a circle around...

1. The loudest dynamic marking: *>*   *mp*   *mf*   *p*   *pp*

2. All dynamic markings softer than *mp*:   *ff*   *p*   *pp*   *mf*   *cresc.*

3. The softest dynamic marking: *mp*   *ff*   *f*   *mf*   *p*

4. Any markings that **gradually** change the volume: *>*   *cresc.*   *pp*   *<*

Exercise 38

Read through this piece of music then answer the questions below.

1. Which drum or cymbal is played the softest? ....

2. In which bar does the music start to gradually get softer? ....

3. Write a dynamic marking at the start of the 2nd bar so that the notes are played very loudly.

4. How many notes should be played moderately loud? ....

5. Draw a symbol just below bar 6 so that the notes gradually get louder.

6. How loud should the hi-hats be played in this piece? ....

Stems

You may have noticed that some notes have their stems up whilst others have their stems down. There is no single rule about which direction to point them so it is best to do whatever makes the music look the clearest.

'All stems up'

Pointing all the stems up can sometimes help to show how notes in a complicated rhythm line-up with each other.

So just remember that there is no right or wrong answer. When writing your own music, point the stems in whichever direction you think makes the music clearest and easiest to read.

Hands and feet

Sometimes it helps to show drums/cymbals that you play with your **hands** with their stems up and drums/cymbals that you play with your **feet** with their stems down.

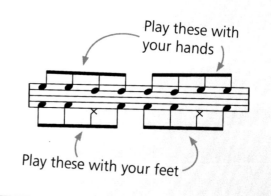

Play these with your hands

Play these with your feet

Exercise 39

As you can see from the examples above, it is quite common to play two or more cymbals or drums at the same time. See if you can name each of these drums and cymbals.

1.

....

....

2.

....

....

3.

....

....

4.

....

....

5.

....

....

6.

....

....

7.

....

....

8.

....

....

....

Accents

One of the more commonly used symbols you will see as a drummer is the **accent**. This looks like an arrow-head and tells you to 'emphasise' the note, or in other words, play it louder than normal so that it 'stands out' from the other notes in the bar.

The last two notes in this rhythm are **accented** and so should be played louder than the others:

How much louder?

There is no exact measure as to how much to emphasise an accented note but a rough guide is to play it one dynamic marking louder than normal. For example, an accented note marked *mf* could be played approximately as if it were marked *f*.

Play! No.5

Don't forget to pay attention to the dynamic markings in these pieces and look out for the accents!

Semiquavers

The next note you need to look at is the **semiquaver**. These look very similar to quavers but they have two tails instead of one.

The next note you need to look at is the **semiquaver**. These look very similar to quavers but they have two tails instead of one.

Out of all the notes you have learnt so far, semiquavers are the shortest.

= ¼ **beat**

Each one lasts for a quarter of a beat.

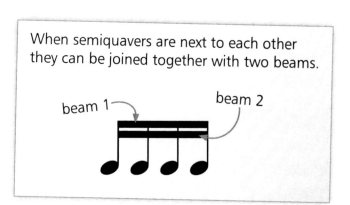

When semiquavers are next to each other they can be joined together with two beams.

Exercise 40

Copy these semiquavers.

1.  COPY

2.  COPY

3.  COPY

4.  COPY

Exercise 41

Fill in the empty boxes to check how well you can remember all the different notes and rests.

What is it called?	Semibreve		Crotchet	Quaver	Semiquaver
What does it look like?	o	𝅗𝅥	♩		
What does its rest look like?				𝄿	𝄿
How long does it last for?	4 beats		1 beat		

You will learn more about these later!

Each semiquaver lasts for a quarter of a beat, so this means that two semiquavers last for half a beat in total:

 = ½ beat

...and four semiquavers last for one whole beat in total:

 = 1 beat

If it helps, think of each crotchet as a biscuit. If you break it in half you get two quavers and if you break it into quarters you get four semiquavers:

1 crotchet   =   2 quavers   =   4 semiquavers

Exercise 42

Add up these fractions.

E.g. ¼ + ¼ = ½

1. ½ + ½ = ...

2. ¼ + ¼ + ¼ + ¼ = ...

3. ¼ + 1 = ...

4. ½ + ¼ = ...

5. 1 + ¼ + ¼ = ...

6. 1 + ½ + ¼ = ...

Exercise 43

Add up the value of these notes to calculate the total number of beats.

 E.g. ♩ + ♪ = 1½ beats

1. = ... beat(s)

2. = ... beat(s)

3. + = ... beat(s)

4. + + = ... beat(s)

5. + = ... beat(s)

6. + = ... beat(s)

Beaming semiquavers

Semiquavers are usually beamed in groups of up to one beat in total and they can also be beamed together with other notes, such as quavers. It is easy to spot which notes are which, as quavers have **one** beam and semiquavers have **two**.

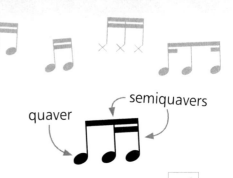

semiquavers

quaver

Exercise 44

Add the missing bar-lines to each of these pieces. Remember that each bar should add up to four beats.

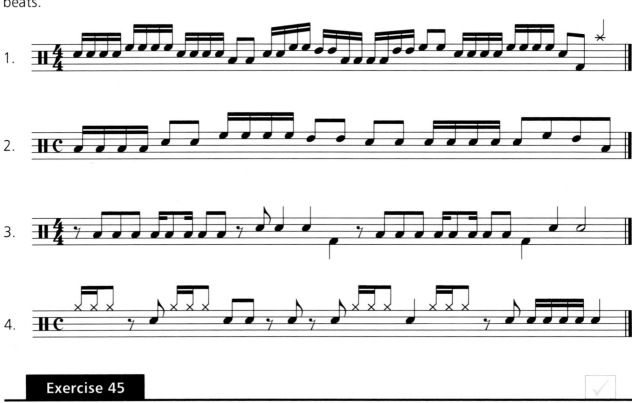

Exercise 45

Fill the gaps with suitable notes or rests from the box. Make sure that each bar lasts for four beats in total.

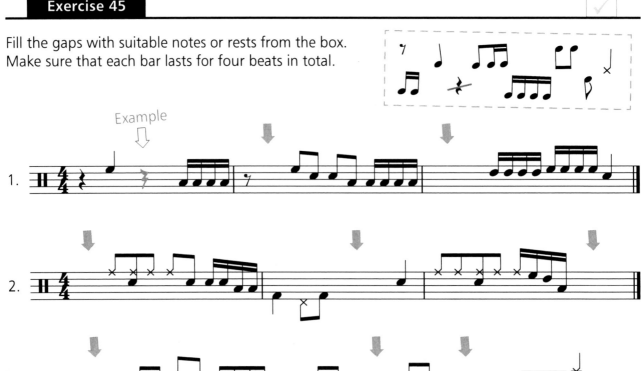

Semiquaver rests

By now you will have probably realised that for each type of note, there is a rest that lasts for the same number of beats.

Semiquaver rest

A **semiquaver rest** lasts for a quarter of a beat. It looks just like a quaver rest, but with an extra curl.

 = a quarter of a beat of silence

Notice how semiquaver rests have two curls and semiquaver notes have two tails or beams.

2 curls   2 tails   2 beams

Exercise 46

Draw some semiquaver rests below. Start like a quaver rest (a), but make the stem (b) a bit longer than normal. Then add an extra dot and curl (c). Use the dots to help you with the first two.

1.   2.   3.   4.

Exercise 47

Fill each gap with a suitable rest from the box.

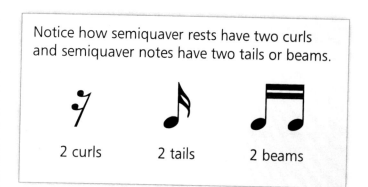
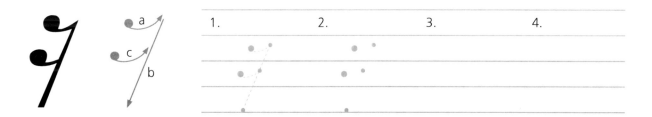

Example

1.

2.

3.

41

These pieces use lots of the notes, rests and symbols that you have learnt so far. Look carefully at the dynamics and tempo markings and always keep counting!

Don't worry if you found these difficult! Book 2 will teach you some more skills and techniques that will help you to count rhythms like the ones above.

Review 3

Well done for reaching the end of the book!

This is the last review piece and it will test you on everything you have learnt so far.
Once you have answered the questions have a go at playing it through.

1.   There are .... minim rests in this piece of music.

2.   Write a metronome mark at the top of the piece.

3.   Add a dynamic marking to the last bar so that it is played very loud.

4.   Fill in the empty bar with notes of your choice - make sure it adds up to four beats!

5.   Draw in the missing rest at the start of bar seven.

6.   Dynamics are usually written .... the stave, whereas tempo

     markings are usually written .... the stave.

7.   The hi-hat with foot is played .... times in this piece.

8.   Draw in the percussion clefs at the beginning of each line.

9.   Four semiquavers last for .... beat(s) in total.

10. Draw in the final bar-line at the end of the piece.

Total

/10

43

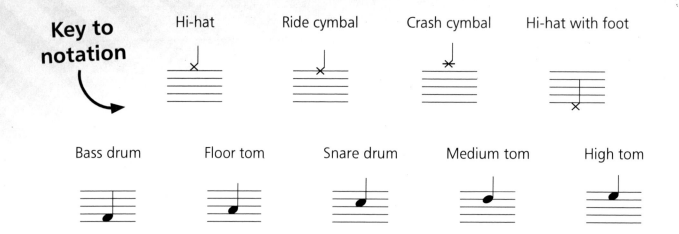

Key to notation

| Hi-hat | Ride cymbal | Crash cymbal | Hi-hat with foot |
| Bass drum | Floor tom | Snare drum | Medium tom | High tom |

Notes and rests

Name	Note	Rest	Duration
Semibreve (also known as 'whole note')	o	▬	4 beats
Minim (also known as 'Half note')	♩	▬	2 beats
Crotchet (also known as 'Quarter note')	♩	⸘	1 beat
Quaver (also known as 'Eighth note')	♪	𝄾	½ beat
Semiquaver (also known as 'Sixteenth note')	♬	𝄿	¼ beat

The names in brackets are
American note names.

Dynamics

Symbol	Italian term	Meaning
ff	fortissimo	very loud
f	forte	loud
mf	mezzo-forte	moderately loud
mp	mezzo-piano	moderately soft
p	piano	soft
pp	pianissimo	very soft
<	crescendo	gradually getting louder
>	diminuendo	gradually getting softer